The Guinea Pigs' Guide to Training Humans

By Charlie Guinea Pig

& Susie Kearley (a.k.a. The Slave)

The Guinea Pigs' Guide to
Training Humans

Cover image: Pixabay

DEDICATION

Dedicated to all the beautiful guinea pigs we've had in our care: Mickey and Rascal, Rodney and Harry, Charlie and Alvin, Merlin and Pumpkin, and little Freddy. These charming squeaky guys have trained us to pander to their every need, to feed them before we feed ourselves, and to go shopping especially for their favourite foods. Nothing is more important than a happy guinea pig.

Signed: *The Slave*

CONTENTS

Humans

Humans are strange creatures, known for making odd sounds and gestures, as well as grabbing and cuddling guinea pigs at the most inconvenient and unreasonable times.
Humans are, however, a reliable source of food, so their presence must be tolerated. Fortunately, they are quite predictable and easy to train. We've put together this book, to help all guinea pigs everywhere, train their humans to cater to their every whim.

PART 1

Part 1 is an instruction manual to help guinea pigs train their humans. It is essential reading for all guinea pigs everywhere.

CHAPTER 1
NATURAL BORN REBEL

Arrival at your adopted home is always a momentous occasion for any guinea pig, but if your human gives you a silly name, you are well within your rights to express your displeasure by ignoring them and hiding. Except when there's food on offer obviously, as this would be counterproductive.

Don't call me Winky!

Start your new relationship as you mean to go on, by squealing for your breakfast at 5am. It is, after all, your duty to wake the whole neighbourhood so the humans all feed their pets. You will be duly rewarded with food - although it may be delayed.

HIDEY HOLES

Hiding places are fun, safe, and they keep life interesting. Be sure to make tents, tunnels, and hidey holes in the most unexpected places. It'll keep your humans entertained and on their toes.

When humans line your hutch with newspaper, this can provide hours of entertainment. It's tasty and makes great tunnels!

If humans use food to tempt you out of hiding. Snatch the food, then run back into your safe place, as quickly as possible.

KEEP THEM ON THEIR TOES!

Humans need to understand your superiority, and their role as your slaves. They must not be allowed to become slackers.

However, humans are fundamentally lazy, so you need to keep them busy. Never allow fresh bedding to stay fresh for long. Make a mess, soil your bedding, demand more hay loudly, and you'll get new bedding, hay and treats served frequently.

*   *   *   *   *   *   *

HOLIDAYS

If your human goes on holiday and leaves you with a pet sitter, remember that the sitter doesn't know how much food you usually get, so you can take advantage of this situation. Adopt a half starved expression, and squeak incessantly until you get more food. By the time you return to your human you'll be so stuffed, you won't have much appetite. They'll give you more of your favourite foods to stimulate your appetite. It's a win: win!

HYPNOSIS

You can hypnotise your humans by looking longingly at them. They find this irresistible. Get them to peer deep into your dark eyes, and they will soon be under your spell. Once you have complete control, you can demand bowls of freshly cut green grass or lush hay.

Try purring at them too - this can have a similar effect, and your hypnotic charms will enable you to get everything you desire.

LONG SUMMER NIGHTS

In the summer, the long evenings are excellent grazing time. Don't let your human put you back in your hutch until sunset. If they want to put you to bed prematurely, give them the run around and evade their grip until they give up.

Assuming they do eventually catch you, after you've had a few more hours grazing time, squeak angrily to make it clear that you aren't happy. Demand additional food, by way of compensation.

CHAPTER 2
UNDERSTANDING HUMAN BEHAVIOUR

When you squeak, your human thinks you're pleased to see them or asking for food. Little do they know that you are hurling insults at them and laughing! They reward you for it, by feeding you treats. Humans really are hilarious creatures.

Be patient with humans. They are simple, foolish creatures, a lesser species. If they're slow to reward you, it's only because they're a bit dim!

GETTING YOUR OWN WAY

Humans need to be loved. This gives you the upper hand. It enables you to manipulate them to get food and treats in return for affection and tolerance.

Stand over your bowl and look at your human longingly. This usually results in fresh food being delivered. Bar biting is another good tactic. It attracts attention and makes you appear close to starvation. It's also so noisy that they'll want to shut you up, so will bribe you with food.

GUINEA PIG SLAVES

Humans clean out your hutch and bedding every day and some humans even refer to themselves as 'guinea pig slaves'. They are quite happy to adopt this subservient position in guinea pig society.

Other humans like to think they are in charge, but their role as cleaner and rubbish man suggests otherwise. Try to be patient with them – humans are not very bright.

Whilst your human is cleaning your hutch, stand in the corner creating a fresh pile of poo. They can barely keep up and it's hilarious!

HUMANS NEED EXERCISE

Never cooperate. When your human says it's time to go into your run, scarper! Give them the runaround for a while. Humans are lazy, and the stretching exercises they engage in, while trying to catch you, are good for their health.

If they put you outside when it's cold, windy, or raining, wee on them when they bring you in, so they learn not to do it again.

TOILET TRAINING

Humans may ask you to poop in a tray. Guinea pigs should never oblige unless being suitably rewarded with a rack full of hay over the toilet, or hand-fed treats whilst doing 'their business'. Scattering your droppings everywhere is a guinea pig's prerogative. Humans must learn to accept that.

Just this once, in return for a full hay rack.

Humans need to know their place as your cleaning staff, cooks, waiting staff, and household servants. They must not become too big for their boots.
Keep them in their place and poop everywhere. It's good for the soul!

TAKE AIM... FIRE!

After you've pooped, do a 'popcorn' and watch the pellets fly everywhere! It's highly entertaining watching your humans trying to clean up after you!

Your human thinks you popcorn because you're happy. Little do they know, you're actually doing it to 'fire' your poops across the room. A little target practice really does make a guinea pig happy!

It's a little known fact among humans that guinea pigs have poop flinging records! You get bonus points for flinging poop directly onto your human or for hitting an item of clothing.

HUMAN GUINEA PIGS

Humans refer to themselves as guinea pigs when they are trying something new. It's an aspirational phrase because they aspire to be more like guinea pigs. But they don't even come close.

CHAPTER 3
MEAL TIMES

There is no such thing as too much food. Guinea pigs should always demand more food, regardless of how much food is in their bowl, how much they have eaten already, whether they stuffed themselves two minutes ago, or whether they are overweight.

Furthermore, there is definitely no such thing as too much carrot or cucumber. All guinea pigs adore carrots and cucumber. Humans worship gods and celebrities. Guinea pigs worship carrots and cucumber.

However, fussiness is every guinea pig's right, and no guinea pig should settle for leftovers. What do they think we are? Second class citizens? Humans should eat the guinea pig leftovers.

So on that note, here are some ideas for getting more, better food...

SELECTIVE EATING

Do not, under any circumstances, eat the brown bits in your muesli. Eat the sweet, brightly coloured bits in your muesli selectively, and leave the rest. This shows your human that you need more food, and better food, and that you're not prepared to compromise. Piggies with savoury preferences can leave the coloured bits instead.

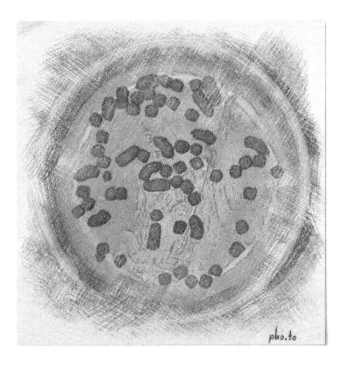

APPEAL TO THEIR SYMPATHIES

One tried and tested approach to getting better food, is to climb up the railings, while hollering loudly. This makes humans think you are:

(a) starving

(b) desperate

(c) cute

Don't let them see the stash of rejected food that you've hidden in the corner of the hutch.

DROPPING HINTS

When your bowl is empty catch your human's attention by behaving badly and noisily. Look at your bowl, look at your human, and then look back at your bowl. Do this until they get the message and serve more food. This might take some time.

MARINADE YOUR FOOD

Food tastes better after it's been dragged across the floor and trodden on. Think of wee as marinade. It helps to bring out the flavour. Be sure to do this to all your food. Also, tip your bowl up so the food goes everywhere. Your slave might then replenish the food bowl, while you holler with laughter in the corner!

SHARING IS CARING

When sharing bowls with your cage mates, remember to block access to the bowl by hogging it or standing in it, so you always get the best pickings. If you have two bowls, be sure to confuse and frustrate your humans by all eating from the same one.

CLEANING TIME!

When being cleaned out, always stand in the way of where your slave is trying to clean. This means you'll be well placed to eat any lost nibbles they unearth.

THE SCALES!

You may suffer the indignity of being weighed. It's embarrassing! Move around on the scales so that it's hard for your humans to get a measurement. Then they'll give up and attempt this less in future.

THE DREADED SYRINGE

If you're feeling off colour and not eating well, your human may produce the dreaded syringe.

If they attempt to syringe feed you, refuse to open your mouth. Do not to take the mush in the syringe, and spit it out if they force you.

Spitting it into their lap is a good idea – it makes their clothes messy and they are less likely to repeat the exercise. Spitting it into their face is even better, if you can project that far!

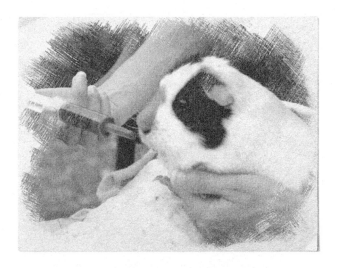

You may have to start eating food which is not to your liking, if you wish to avoid the dreaded syringe, regardless of how off colour you're feeling.

CHAPTER 4
MAKING THE SLAVES WORK

Some days when you're feeling lazy and can't be bothered to eat, don't exert yourself. Just look longingly at your human and they will try to help. It is a great way to get hand-fed your favourite foods, in large quantities, with less effort on your part.

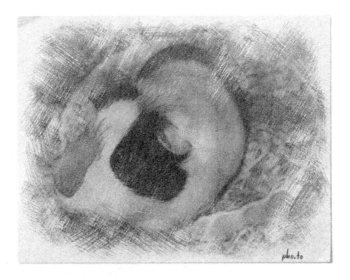

* * * * * * *

HAVE A LIE IN

When you can't be bothered to get out of bed in the morning, humans think this is funny. Unless you appear to be dead. Then they start behaving strangely and making odd noises.

Once they have ascertained that you are not dead, humans will be delighted to provide breakfast on demand. They may also be delighted that you had a lie in, as there was no 5am wake-up call.

MAKE THEM WAIT ON YOU

If you can't be bothered to eat the grass from the lawn because breaking the blade is too much effort, then demand cut grass by squeaking loudly. You might get treats and dandelion leaves first (humans aren't very intelligent) but who's complaining!

PLAN A PARTY

Whilst you're snuggled up in your cosy bed, you can be planning the antics of the days and nights ahead. Invite your wild rodent friends round.

Pull your hay rack off the wall, turn your food and water upside down, empty your bedroom of bedding, and camp under the stars, enjoying all the fun of a wild party.

There is no need to spare a thought for the human who is going to come and clear up your mess in the morning. That's their role in life. They enjoy being enslaved by you.

Sleep off the party mood the next day – the humans won't notice.

PARTYING INDOORS

If your noisy antics wake the household at night, the humans may think they have burglars downstairs. If they come to investigate, act chilled and nonchalant until they've reassured themselves that it's just the guinea pig turning his hutch upside down, and plod wearily back upstairs to sleep.

LATE NIGHT SNACKS

It's perfectly acceptable to occasionally wake your humans at 2am by shrieking for snacks. They will be pleased to come and feed you in the early hours of the morning.

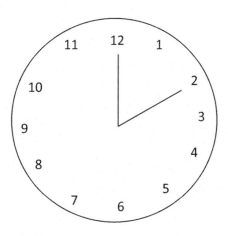

THE FOOD BOWL

Always poop and wee in the food bowl. This ensures your bowl is washed before the next meal. You don't want the staff to start slacking!

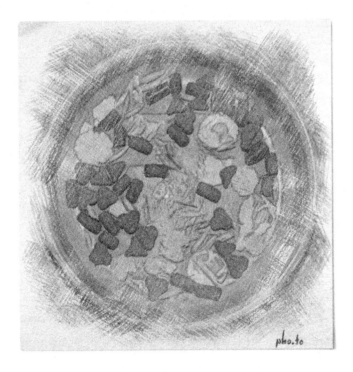

CHAPTER 5
AT THE VET

Avoid the vet at all costs. If you are feeling under the weather, grin and bear the discomfort, and hopefully no-one will notice you're off colour.

BEWARE OF THE GLASS OBJECT!

If you do have to go to the vet, watch out for the cold glass thing that gets stuck up your bottom! Squeal and wriggle at the sight of it! Humans think this measuring device is helpful, but it's indecent. Be sure to fart, poop, and wee on it, so it slips out prematurely.

BEWARE SHAMPOO!

If you hear the word lice or mites, watch out. You might get a stinky lotion on the back of your neck, or worse – you might get shampooed!

If you're really annoyed, it's perfectly acceptable to nip the vet's finger. Be sure to wee on him at every opportunity and leave plenty of poops behind.

THE UPSIDE OF APPETITE LOSS

Losing your appetite has one perk: your human might offer you a syringe full of strawberry flavour Complan (after you've rejected that yucky stuff from the vet - see 'the dreaded syringe' above).

This is the one and only occasion when syringes are good. Complan is delicious and you should slurp it up enthusiastically. Quickly demonstrate that you are feeling better so that you don't need antibiotics, glass objects, or other unpleasantries.

Susie Kearley

CHAPTER 6
HUTCH ETIQUETTE

Humans don't understand the thrills of fighting, so only fight with your cage mate when your human isn't looking.

Don't let your human catch you fighting frequently because they might cut your privates off!

CHEWING ETIQUETTE

It is courteous to chew anything you can get your teeth into – wooden or plastic. This shows your human that you appreciate the item – unless you are chewing the bars on your cage, which indicates desperate hunger or a desire to escape. Either way, the outcome is beneficial. By destroying your toys, you will get new toys, and by chewing your railings, you may get food treats or larger accommodation. Chewing is generally good and brings rewards.

Chewing doors and furniture however, can get you banished from the house, so there may be exceptions.

DEMAND SPACIOUS ACCOMMODATION

If you feel your accommodation is too small, pace back and forth, trying to escape whenever the door is opened. This will make you look bored and frustrated, which may compel your human to provide larger accommodation and better entertainment.

ZOOMIES

Humans are simple creatures who enjoy watching guinea pigs zooming around. So another tactic for getting more space is to play zoomies frequently. Your humans will naturally want to give you ample space to run around in if you show you're enjoying the space. They're also more likely to spend time feeding you treats if you're lively and entertaining.

PERSONAL SPACE

If your cage mate is getting on your nerves, and you want a period of separation, try cowering in the corner of your hutch and limping. You may be separated for a while. Alternatively, chatter your teeth at your cage mate, which may have the same effect.

CHAPTER 7
DUBIOUS PLEASURES

MODELLING

If your human points a camera at you, run way until they offer you tasty treats – your cooperation as a photographic model should always be paid for with treats.

pho.to

BATHS

If you hear the word 'bath', hide! If your human catches you, they may cover you in disgusting smelling soap, place you in horrible yucky water and you may drown. Plus it can take weeks to recoup that attractive guinea pig fragrance, which you've worked so hard to perfect! Wriggling, jumping, biting, and screaming are all recommended strategies to help keep baths to an absolute minimum.

HARNESSES

When your human tries to put you in a harness, squeal, wriggle, and complain like billy-oh. This behaviour is very much justified, as the use of harnesses on guinea pigs is inappropriate.

The benefit of wriggling and complaining, is that your human will either ensure it is a loose fit (so you escape) or give up altogether.

If they succeed in putting the harness on, bolt for the nearest bush. You are now safe to wriggle free and hide. Your head is smaller than your neck, so harnesses are invariably a poor fit, making it easy to escape.

This leaves your human standing in the garden with a lead into the bushes. Meanwhile you're munching through the greens on their vegetable plot.

NAIL CLIPPERS

At the first sight of nail clippers hide! These evil devices are designed to ruin your beautiful claws and should be banned!

INDOOR GUINEA PIGS & HEROS

Pay particular attention to television programmes of guinea pigs. The G Force movie shows that you have the potential to be a superhero. Practise your superhero skills around the house, taking care not to hurt yourself. Remember that even in G Force, guinea pigs cannot fly. It is important to remember this when attempting to leap from the arms of a human, or escape from a table top.

DESTRUCTIVE GUINEA PIGS

When your human lets you out of the hutch to run about in the lounge, you will probably inspect everything - chew wires, nibble furniture, test the area behind the sofa as a hiding place and toilet. Hard to reach areas like this, make excellent dens. Your human will start to put newspaper-lined hidey boxes in your favourite places. But don't push your luck - there are limits to your human's tolerance of guinea pig induced destruction!

Me? destructive? Never!

MAKING FRIENDS

Do not trust cats. They might seem friendly, but they can turn nasty.

Pigeons and other birds are harmless, but watch for the birds of prey who could pose a risk to your safety in an open top run. Best run for cover, if your human is stupid enough not to provide proper security.

Squirrels will steal your food given half the chance - ours ran off with the squirrel-proof bird feeder!

Beware of dogs and foxes. They might appear docile, but they are not your friends.

Small humans may try to pick you up. This can be stressful, so run, hide, and squeal. If they succeed, pee and poop on them - with any luck, they'll put you down again.

Avoid small humans with water pistols / hosepipes.

Avoid larger humans if they are walking funny, speaking slurred or appear to be inebriated in any other way. They are not in control of their faculties.

THE MODELS

The models in this section are:

Charlie

Likes cucumber, carrot, hay, guinea pig sweeties,
his toilet, and his cosy bed.

Dislikes the green bits in his muesli.

MODEL

Alvin

Likes anything Charlie will let him have from the food bowl, and cosying up with Charlie in a single pigloo.

Dislikes loud noises and being startled.

MODELS

Rodney and Harry

Like carrot peelings, guinea pig sweeties, spinach, fresh grass, and each other, but only in small doses.

Dislike cauliflower, being handled, and brown bits in their muesli.

MODELS

Merlin and Pumpkin

Like fresh greens, broccoli, fresh grass, and they are very much in lurve.

Dislike sudden noises and food from the local pet shop.

PART 2

This section is a collection of my articles that have been published in magazines on the topic of guinea pigs

CHAPTER 8

CHARLIE GUINEA PIG GOES CAMPING

Charlie guinea pig wasn't eating much or drinking anything following treatment for an abscess in June, so he needed syringe feeding, regular watering, probiotics, and intensive care. I'm fortunate to work from home, so I could attend to his needs throughout the day.

However, we had a two-week holiday booked and didn't know what to do about Charlie. After much deliberation, we were planning to leave him with a lady who runs a local guinea pig rescue, and offers boarding while owners take holidays. She was aware of his condition, and said she'd do her best.

But we weren't 100% confident with this plan. We were experiencing a heatwave, she works all day, and I was worried that if the hot weather continued, Charlie would dehydrate while she was out at work. He wouldn't get regular watering by syringe throughout the day.

The night before we went away, it was decision time. We decided to take Charlie with us to Wales.

We just couldn't leave him with someone else while his health needs were so critical. How were we going to climb Snowdon and still meet Charlie's needs? We hadn't quite worked that out yet.

Deciding what to do about Charlie

In the week running up to the day we left, we were still undecided. My husband, Vic, was worried that children would interfere with Charlie on the campsites. Charlie doesn't like being handled - he's old, fragile, and wasn't very well. Dogs or foxes could pose a problem, so good security measures would be critically important. We were keen to ensure he was protected from extreme temperatures too.

In anticipation that we might want to take Charlie camping, I made enquiries with the three campsites we'd booked into. "Can I bring my guinea pig? Is there enough shade if this heatwave continues? Is there somewhere secure, safe and shady where we can leave his hutch (away from curious young campers) if we need to do so during the day?"

The campsites reassured me that there were plenty of options and we could work it out when we got there. One even offered to keep him safe in a locked, no-go area where the gas supplies are stored.

So we took Charlie guinea pig on holiday and he made a miraculous recovery! We fitted a padlock to the hutch and took a run that he could use on the grass, under our supervision. He's doing well now. Here is his story...

Bedgellert

The experience began with a six hour journey to Bedgellert in Snowdonia. I tried to offer Charlie reassurance by keeping him on my lap, but it became apparent after an hour, that he wanted to get up and walk about, so he went into his carry case, walked about a bit, and then settled down. Despite all our concerns that the journey might be stressful for him, he took it in his stride and seemed remarkably chilled out about the journey.

He had food and water available. I gave him a syringe feed half way, and he was starting to sip from his drinking bottle for the first time in about a week, which was fabulous!

The first site however, wasn't well suited to guinea pigs. We'd been so worried about the heatwave that we hadn't thought much about rain. I'd checked the forecast, but it hadn't predicted downpours.

That weekend, it rained and rained and rained. We raised the hutch off the ground and replaced the bedding twice a day. Fortunately Vic packed some plastic sheeting, mainly to keep the wind off, but it served to keep the rain off too. I was now worried that Charlie would be affected by the midges. I was being eaten alive!

We wanted to climb Snowdon, and had joked about taking Charlie up in a baby carrier, so we could water him en route - but I'm sure he wouldn't have liked that, so we didn't! The problem went away: it was so cold that heat wasn't a problem, and Charlie started drinking for himself, so we felt it was OK to leave him for the duration of the climb. We only got half way up the mountain before heavy cloud and pelting rain forced us to retreat anyway! It was supposed to clear in the afternoon! Oh well. Hello Charlie! We're back!

The campsite was in the forest, so there were lots of trees, but no lawn for Charlie's run. And nowhere to dry out after all that rain! He stayed in the hutch eating handfuls of grass, but we weren't sorry to move on to Anglesey after three days in rainy Snowdonia!

Anglesey

Charlie was now an expert at travel and happily journeyed for an hour in his carry case. When he arrived at Anglesey, he was very excited: vast lawns of lush green grass awaited him. The sun was out. He was squeaking to get out, and we set up his run before anything else. Charlie was in heaven, keeping the campsite lawn in check.

We were booked into the Anglesey campsite for a week, and actually stayed for eight days because Charlie loved it so much, and so did we!

But the weather continued to be awful! The sunshine gave way to days of rain and I was lying awake at night hoping Charlie was OK in his hutch, covered in plastic sheeting, as the rain hammered down outside! I'd have brought him into the caravan, except Vic's allergic to him so that wouldn't have worked!

When Vic started thrashing around in bed at night, I threatened to send him to sleep in the car and bring Charlie into the caravan instead!

Then one evening, during Charlie's syringe feeding session, he was wheezing and I thought he'd picked up a respiratory infection in all the damp weather. I was cursing my stupidity for *not* leaving him at home with the lady who runs the rescue centre.

That night, I popped him into his carry case and put him in the car for the night, to ensure he wasn't exposed to any more damp air. In the morning he was fine. No wheezing. Thank goodness.

Towards the end of the week the weather brightened up again, and Charlie was out in his run, loving the lawn, while we supervised. We booked an extra day so Charlie could enjoy the lawn and we could see more of the Anglesey coast in sunny weather!

Mount Tryfan

Our last stop was a campsite at the foot of Tryfan in Snowdonia. It was cheap and basic, so we weren't sure what to expect. It turned out to be quite an experience! The farmer had free range chickens, ducks and sheep roaming around the campsite. When one of the chickens took a liking to Charlie's left-overs, it made them seem much more attractive! There's nothing like a bit of competition to stimulate the appetite.

The grass was taller than Charlie, and the views across the mountains of Snowdonia were fabulous, although we're not sure if Charlie appreciated them. The midges weren't too bad, although I think we'd all had enough of them by departure day.

Would we take Charlie camping again? I think it's better for the guinea pig to leave him with a caring and responsible adult while you're away, but if he had critical care needs, I would do it again.

There are risks, but I was better able to prioritise Charlie's care needs than anyone at home. I didn't have confidence in my mum's syringe feeding skills, and I wanted to be there if Charlie needed me. It was lovely to see him regain his appetite and enjoy the lawns.

Key considerations for travelling with a sick guinea pig

Be prepared for all kinds of weather: We had major hutch operations going on to keep the weather out, with plastic sheeting on all sides, and wooden blocks to raise the hutch off the ground. Rocks and sheets of wood helped to hold the plastic sheeting in place. When it was sunny, we also needed to ensure he had shade, so we created a make-shift tent over his hutch, to provide shade on a hot day.

Security is a top priority: A sick guinea pig will probably not appreciate being interfered with by well-meaning children. We fitted a padlock and chain to the hutch before we left and *never* left him in the run unsupervised. We also tried to hide the hutch from view, as much as possible, when we were out during the day.

Will your host allow pets? I made phone calls to all the campsites to check on whether guinea pigs were allowed, whether there was enough shade if the heatwave continued, and whether there was a secure place for the hutch if necessary.

What to do when you go out: We pitched near a tall hedge whenever possible, for shade, and then put the hutch in a shady spot around the back of the caravan, beside the hedge. This meant the hutch was mostly obscured from view and was unlikely to attract attention. We didn't want Charlie disturbed while we were out. When there was no hedge and it was sunny, we constructed a shady make-shift tent to protect him from overheating! See 'weather' above.

Protection from predators: A sturdy hutch, when closed properly, should keep dogs and other predators out. Our padlock and chain provided extra security, mostly to keep inquisitive children out. But it added a degree of protection from clever hounds too! We put the run, which is heavy, in front of the hutch so even if a dog did discover the hutch, he wouldn't be able to get close to Charlie.

Travelling conditions: Animals like to be able to move about when travelling, so do ensure they have access to a good size carry case, with food and water available on demand. Be prepared to make breaks in the journey to attend to your pet's needs.

A local vet: It's good to find out where the nearest vet is in case of an emergency. We needed to find one when hungry Charlie nearly ran out of his syringe food. The vet rectified the situation and all was well.

Recommendation: I'd always recommend leaving a small vulnerable animal with a responsible carer while you're away. However, desperate times do call for drastic measures occasionally. It's been interesting, but perhaps not the most relaxing holiday ever!

What's next?

Charlie has recovered beautifully. He has a good appetite and is drinking plenty. There's still that pesky abscess, which we'll manage with help from the vet. For now at least, Charlie is happy.

CHAPTER 9

ANIMAL CRACKERS! LIFE'S AN ADVENTURE!

It's hard to imagine anyone getting as excited about food, as my guinea pigs get about a dandelion leaf. Presented with a whole plant, they squeak with delight, go running round the cage, jumping, and spend all afternoon nibbling and playing with it. It honestly begs the question why anyone would bother with children, when these beautiful little fellas are so delightful, grateful, obedient, and easy to please.

Let me introduce Harry and Rodney, two brothers (we think - but haven't undertaken DNA testing), who were found wandering around Milton Keynes on their own, with ear infections. We like to envisage them in the shopping centre, complete with shopping bags having a great time. But in reality, they were scrawny, hungry, infected and not very happy at all. So someone took them to the RSPCA centre at Blackberry Farm in Aylesbury, where they met us.

Now I would like to say 'the rest is history', but that's not quite true. The story continues... little

Harry, the bravest (and fattest) of the two, decided last spring that he 'fancied' Rodney. We couldn't quite believe what we were seeing, as Harry mounted Rodney and started thrusting his hips! Quick action needed!

Poor little Rodney was brought inside, whilst we tried to figure out if we actually had 'Rodnetta' on our hands. With his bottom turned up and compared against pictures of guinea pig genitals on our computer screen, we came to the conclusion that yes, we think Rodney is definitely a boy. So what to do about the over-excited guinea pig outside?

We separated the two for a few days. Harry looked upset - he'd been having a great time! The separation approach continued until Harry learnt to behave - which didn't take long, because Harry didn't like being on his own.

Different entertainment presented itself when Harry made friends with a cat. He climbs up the railings to say 'hello' every time the cat passes. The cat thinks Harry looks delicious, but cannot get to him, so the two have a relationship of mutual appreciation!

Harry and Rodney live next to a pond which attracts two ducks most of the time, but occasionally other males arrive and batchelor parties occur - splashing, chasing and generally having a good time. If the lady duck is around these parties have been known to degenerate into a full blown orgie.

During the winter, Rodney and Harry made friends with a mouse - a wild mouse who lived in the garage with them, and would eat from their breakfast bowl! Mr Mouse was an amazing gymnast! He could squeeze through the bars of the guinea pig 'hotel', even though the bars are a fraction of his waist size - it was quite incredible to watch! Rodney and Harry haven't learnt to do that fortunately.

However, we did have a guinea pig called Micky Houdini once. Micky had a miraculous way of escaping from his harness and disappearing into the garden undergrowth. The harnesses were never very successful. The piggies weren't keen on them, and despite being sold for guinea pigs, they're not much use for animals whose face is slimmer than their neck! Herewith ends the story of our guinea pigs, as the happy little fellas are waiting patiently outside for their tea!

CHAPTER 10

DIARY OF A WIMPY GUINEA PIG

"Go away!" squeaked Rodney as he cowered at the back of his hutch looking fearfully at me. He wanted to eat his breakfast, but wasn't coming out whilst I was standing there. "Leave me to eat in peace!" he whimpered.

As I walked away, I felt sorry for my wimpy guinea pig. Rodney is scared. He is frightened of me, my husband and everything around him. So when I saw a Bach flower remedy for timid pets in a shop, I thought of Rodney. Could a flower essence really make my wimpy guinea pig brave?

Rodney and his brother Harry were adopted from the RSPCA in 2010. A couple of years later, following a period of sickness, Harry died leaving soul mate Rodney, on his own. We tried to find him a new friend but they weren't getting on.

Perhaps I was expecting too much when I bought a Bach Flower remedy for Rodney and his new companion, and expected it to transform the terrible fighting twosome into best friends. I had hoped they might start gurgling happily, but instead, my small furry boys were chattering their teeth and growling at one another. This was clearly not a match made in heaven.

The products

'Bioforce Animal Timid Essence' was the first blend to capture my imagination, but I was uncomfortable about giving Rodney alcohol and was concerned that twelve drops of 27% alcohol might (a) not taste very nice, (b) not agree with his liver, (c) make him tipsy!

So eventually I settled on Nelson's Rescue Remedy for Pets, an alcohol-free solution, which contains a number of different flower essences to help Rodney with his confidence and reduce his levels of fear and stress. As two guinea pigs now needed treatment, I hoped it would it help them both to relax!

One of the first things I noticed when I placed my order online, was that the reviews for this remedy on Amazon were very good! People who had bought it for frightened dogs and cats had apparently seen a remarkable transformation! The leaflet says that the calming effect is supposed to be immediate. So it was with a degree of eager anticipation, combined with a healthy dose of scepticism, that the trial began.

Alternative Bach flower remedies include:

- Bioforce Animal Timid Essence
- The Bach Centre individual remedies
- Pet Lovers Digest Flower Essence Blends

Rodney's diary

By the time the Rescue Remedy arrived in the post, we'd already had three days of conflict with Rodney and his new companion bickering and fighting. So we had great hopes for the treatment. Rodney was stressed out and being chased around by the new guinea pig. The day before, Rodney had been the bully, but today the newcomer was dominant. They both needed to chill!

Rescue remedy Trial - Day one

I gave both guinea pigs three 4-drop doses of Rescue Remedy in the morning, noon and night. A wire mesh was put between them for most of the day. They continued to chatter their teeth and show aggression all morning but had worn themselves out by the afternoon. The barrier was removed and within minutes the newcomer was chasing Rodney around the hutch. It ended in a furry entanglement on the floor. Rodney ran upstairs (the newcomer couldn't master the ramp).

Day two

On the second day, Rescue Remedy was given to both guinea pigs and early conflict was followed by remarkable tranquillity in the afternoon as the twosome tolerated each other's presence. However, before supper was served, Rodney was chased around mercilessly, and ran to the upper floor for some peace. He hadn't exercised so much in years!

Day three

Rescue Remedy didn't stop the unhappy antics in the guinea pig cage. Separations followed by reintroductions weren't working. They had been together for 6 days by now, and the lady from the rescue centre said they should have bonded if they were going to, so she collected Rodney's companion that afternoon. Rodney smiled.

A week later

Having given Rodney a week to get over the ordeal, he was gurgling and squeaking happily. He'd had a break from companions, and from Rescue Remedy, but I wanted to see if the flower essence would give him confidence around me. The effect is supposed to be immediate and there is no accumulated benefit from prolonged use – in fact, the benefit reduces over time. So when drops on his breakfast were followed by permission to stroke his nose, I tentatively wondered if we'd made a breakthrough! Rodney usually bolts at the sight of my hand.

Day 11

Permission to stroke the nose was granted again! But without the aid of Rescue Remedy. Is Rodney just becoming more human-friendly after his guinea pig ordeal? Maybe he's getting lonely in the absence of Harry.

Day 12

Rodney's escaped! As I turned the hutch upside down looking for my cute little fella, little did I realise that he was standing behind a chair looking back at me! My antics stressed him out so much, he disappeared into hiding for the rest of the day. Sorry Rodney.

Day 13 and beyond

I tested the Rescue Remedy in a variety of situations this week and cannot say I noticed any change in his behaviour. I gave him drops on his breakfast and dinner to see if it made him less afraid of me. It didn't.

He was too frightened to take food from my hand, so I added the treatment to food in his bowl and went away. I returned later and he still wouldn't take treats from me, but he ate them when I'd gone!

So I'm afraid I have to conclude, that this particular Bach flower remedy has failed to make my wimpy guinea pig brave! Maybe I need a different blend!

My theory

Food is comforting – we all know that – and Bach Flower remedies for pets are designed to be dropped onto food. This means that when your stressed pet gets his remedy, he is getting some comforting food with it. I think the food may influence behaviour more than the flower essence, but until someone conducts a double-blind clinical trial, I guess we'll never know!

Tips for people with wimpy guinea pigs

These tips have been suggested by Laura Humphreys from the Guinea Pig Helpline. She's a qualified Rodent Health Advisor with the British Association of Rodentologists.

1. Aim to handle your guinea pigs little and often – a few minutes two or three times a day is a good way to start, you can build on the length of time handled as they settle down.

2. Holding some food for them to eat while they are on your lap is one way to encourage their trust in you.

3. When they are exercising in their run, try laying out tunnels and places to hide. This will help them feel secure and arouse their curiosity.

4. Exercise and movement can be encouraged by spreading their daily fresh fruit and vegetables around the cage or floor area, rather than serving them in a dish.

5. There is no need to tiptoe around them but do talk to them when approaching their cage and while you are around them. This will be comforting to them and boost their confidence.

6. It is normal even for confident piggies to run from you when you try to catch them. Gently and calmly herd them into a hiding place or corner of the cage before lifting with both hands.

7. When you lift your guinea pigs out of their cage, or place them back inside, always ensure they are facing towards you. If they are facing forwards there is a danger that they will jump from your grip and this is one of the main causes of accidents.

8. Decide on a rough routine and stick to it so they learn what to expect from you. For example, you might decide to clean their cage every morning and provide fresh vegetables every dinner time.

9. Make sure they are living in suitable groups of two or more — guinea pigs usually thrive on company of their own kind! Young ones especially, will be very timid if they are living alone.

10. Have patience and understand that it will take time for them to fully settle. They will get there if you persevere gently but firmly with the above tips!

CHAPTER 11

PAINTING GUINEA PIGS IS MY PASSION

Caroline Whittle is a painter and illustrator with a passion for guinea pigs and other small furry pets. She studied at the Berkshire College of Art and Design, and since graduating with an HND, has enjoyed a long career in the greeting card industry. Susie Kearley asked her about her pets and her paintings.

"I have four guinea pigs: Lola, Ruby, Coco-Cappuccino and Steve-O," says Caroline, "They're all individuals. Lola waits in the corner of the pen by my 'relaxing' chair with her nose in the air if she wants something. Ruby is very gentle and shy, but totally in love with Steve-O and it's mutual. She licks his face, but also barbers his wonderful 'skirt'! Is that caring love, possessiveness or making him look less hot for the other ladies? I'm not sure!

"Their favourite foods are cucumber, grass, hay, celery, greens, tomatoes and carrots. Ruby adores pears. The clamour for their morning cucumber has to be seen to be believed and the wheeking cacophony, and desperate climbing up the pen sides, when they smell fresh grass is a joy to behold! This is how they train me.

"They do have some bad habits too though! They strip down their cardboard chewable huts when I'm trying to watch TV or sleep! They're always seeking out wires and plastic, so I have to be very vigilant before I let them out for a run. Ruby 'trimming' Steve-O's hair is not good, either!

"They live in a hutch made from coroplast/cubes system. Interlocking grids are connected to fit the available surface area and it's lined with a corrugated plastic liner for easy cleaning. This is coated with a thick layer of newspaper, with either hay or fleece on top. Their pen is on a table at waist-height in my studio. They have 'bunkbeds' with fleece, but hay in their cardboard caves.

"A couple of my previous guinea pigs, Rusty and Liam, had the run of an enclosed sunken living area in my house. When people visited, they soon learned that if they begged, they'd get treats. The funniest thing was that they managed to leap up onto the sofa and that was where I'd find them in the morning! Soiling wasn't a problem as guinea pigs like to go to the toilet in dark places - usually their beds. It was a truly wonderful experience, especially at Christmas when we put the presents under the tree. Rusty and Liam were right there, climbing on top of them. They were very excited!

"I was eight years old when I got my first guinea pig. I used to look after the school animals and had been promised that I could look after Soda, the school guinea pig, for the summer holidays. Then the teacher let someone else have him and I was devastated. My mum heard about some piggies needing homes and so my first guinea pig, William, was mine four weeks later. He had a VERY unconventional life! It was a short walk along a quiet country lane to school and we would go together, with him trotting along beside me!

"I usually have rescues or unwanted guinea pigs. This means they come into my life when they need me and I give them a wonderful forever home. I love all the different breeds, but I am very partial to pink-eyed goldens. I had two very special boys, Lester and Chester of that breed. They were fiesty individuals!

"Chester was an angry young guinea pig who wouldn't be held at any cost. When I parted from my partner at the time, I was sat on the floor in my studio crying. Chester was out for a run, and unbelievably he climbed onto my lap, stretched out and let me stroke him. When I was calm again, he turned and looked at me, as if to say 'Are you alright now?' Then jumped off. That was the end of his sympathies!

"Later that year, I noticed he had flaky, itchy skin that didn't clear up after veterinary treatment. He then developed a cough. I was lucky to have bought the revolutionary new book, 'The proper care of guinea pigs' by Peter Gurney. He'd listed his telephone number for emergencies and I called him. He informed me that Chester probably had systemic mycosis (a fungal skin problem that had progressed to his internal organs) and that he would die without anti-fungal treatment. I drove to London that evening and Peter treated Chester, successfully. As a thank you, I painted his best-loved late guinea pig, Doddy. That was my first ever guinea pig painting, astonishingly! I suppose before, I'd always painted whatever I was asked to paint.

"Peter was delighted with the painting and sent me a beautiful bouquet of flowers with a card saying that 'through my eyes and hands, Doddy had come home'. We both cried when I spoke to him later.

"Since my first little guinea pig, William, joined me when I was eight, I've had the pleasure of keeping over forty guinea pigs. All of them were lovely and adorable. Some were real characters. Findley, a guinea pig given to me by Peter, was the model for my first 'Out of the Hutch!' painting. He was so cheeky and wilful. He lived downstairs, free-range, and actually climbed the stairs to come to my studio at the time, where the girl guinea pigs were. His climbing antics inspired my painting of a skiing piggy! I looked at his cheeky face and suddenly saw him all togged up in winter attire skiing. The painting was done in three hours and I had never enjoyed creating anything as much as I did that first whimsical portrait.

"I used that image for my business Christmas card that year, and it was followed by many more paintings of guinea pigs in action. I wanted to be able to buy cards with guinea pig images on them, but there was nothing available. So having produced this beautiful picture of Doddy for Peter, and then one of Findley skiing, I decided to produce a full range of guinea pig paintings, showing them doing all sorts of different things. The Flying Carpet image is my most iconic design.

"I started attending guinea pig shows to display my paintings and sell greetings cards. Among the most memorable of these was The Guinea Pig Extravaganza in Virginia, USA. I realised that adults keeping guinea pigs was much more mainstream in the US, and people were really open and enthusiastic about it. Back in the UK, in 1999, it was considered rather eccentric for adults to keep guinea pigs, because they were regarded as children's pets. In the US, they loved what I was doing, while in the UK, they seemed to think it was a bit weird. So I started to feel more at home in the USA!

"In February 2000, I took my portfolio of work to the annual greeting card fair at Birmingham NEC. There was a resounding no-vote from the eminent publishers who unanimously agreed that only cats, dogs and mainly bears were cute, not guinea pigs. 'They don't have the ahhh factor', I was told.

"So I decided that my market was indeed the USA. I sold my house in Woodley, Berkshire and then rented on the Isle of Wight so I could spend time with my family, while I investigated how I might be able to achieve a viable income from a website advertising myself and my work, if I were to emigrate to the USA.

"I also concentrated on writing and illustrating children's books to present to an American publisher. I spent a month in Mississippi with friends, building contacts and attending a Southern Breeze children's writing seminar in Alabama. It was October 2003, and I planned to return the following summer to publish the books, but sadly, this was not to be. Hurricane Katrina wreaked devastation on the Deep South, destroying the lives of thousands of people. It marked the end of my business plan for America, which, of course was inconsequential in comparison.

"I turned my attention to charity fundraising here in the UK. I set up a website and sold my own greeting cards and high-quality prints online. I took commissions to paint pet portraits to broaden my portfolio, and that went well. I was keeping pretty busy.

"Then in 2006, I had a sudden shock that took it's toll on my health. My good friend and guinea pig guru, Peter Gurney, passed away. His death had a huge impact on me. I was devastated and felt very low. I then contracted the Epstein-Barr virus, which developed into ME, leaving me exhausted all the time, with no option but to fold the business.

"Today, I'm still recovering, and it's been a long, slow journey back to health, but I'm full of new ideas and raring to go. I'm taking a new look at my children's stories and rewriting them from a fresh perspective.

"While I was ill, some days all I could do was lay in a dark room. My world became a very small place, lived at a very slow pace. I spent a lot of time in the restful stillness of the company of my guinea pigs. It inspired me to create my 'Picnic at Coleman's Farm' painting, where the rabbits and guinea pigs living in a petting zoo take some time out after a stressful day.

"If I had done more of that, I doubt if I would've become ill. I find painting small furry animals very therapeutic. These days I pace myself and find being in a magical world of innocence, beauty, and magic is where I want to be. The world has moved on and now there are guinea pig images everywhere. I like to think I played some part in that.

"Among my special commissions was a piece of art entitled 'Autumn Pannage'. My client wanted all of the guinea pigs she and her husband had ever rescued in one painting, including their two bunnies and their dog, in an autumnal setting."

View Caroline's stores of beautiful guinea pig themed items on the links below...

www.redbubble.com/people/outofthehutch/shop

www.etsy.com/market/out_of_the_hutch

CHAPTER 12

WILD GUINEA PIGS

We typically think of guinea pigs as pets, but their close cousins, wild cavies, still live freely in parts of South America, from where the species originates. Guinea pigs, the domestic variety, don't exist naturally in the wild, but they are descendants of a closely related species of wild cavy, probably the montane guinea pig, Cavia tschudii.

Wild cavies aren't as colourful or interesting to look at as many of the guinea pigs we have as pets. This is because our pet guinea pigs have been selectively bred over thousands of years, for their pretty colours and fancy coats.

Wild cavies are relatively plain in appearance, often agouti brown. They blend into nature, which is just as well, because they're prey animals, so it helps them survive. They live in the Andes mountains and grasslands of Brazil, Uruguay, Argentina, and Peru. The montane guinea pig, thought to be the domestic guinea pig's most likely ancestor, lives at around 2,000 to 3,800 metres above sea level, and enjoys moist rocky habitats, with rough vegetation.

Some species of 'wild' cavy, such as C. anolaimae and C. guianae, were first identified in the 20th century, and are thought to be the feral descendents of domestic guinea pigs who were reintroduced into the wild.

Wild cavies might live for between one and four years. While this isn't usually as long as their domesticated cousins, wild cavies have amazing freedoms to roam in beautiful mountainous and grasslands, but with the obvious risk of being caught by predators.

Wild cavies are herbivores like domestic guinea pigs. They stick together, grazing on vegetation, and find shelter in the burrows of other animals, as well as hiding among rocks and in vegetation. This instinct to hide has been passed on to domestic guinea pigs, who are naturally drawn towards tunnels and hiding places. Wild cavies create routes through the foliage, and eat leaves, grasses, clovers, and some flowers.

They live in family groups, usually including a number of sows, a single boar, and their young. Wild guinea pigs tend to be most active at dawn and dusk, perhaps because in the bright sunshine of daytime, they're more vulnerable to predation.

Animals that pose a threat to wild cavies include snakes, wild cats, owls, coyotes, wolves, and humans. The predators eat them, while the humans are a threat on many levels. In some countries, guinea pigs and cavies are considered to be a healthy meat for human consumption. But humans are also a threat because cavies are taken from the wild for the pet trade, or for breeding. Humans are also prone to destroying habitats, as we well know.

Some practitioners of traditional folk medicine in the Andes mountains, think wild cavies can help them to identify the cause of disease by squealing at the source of the illness in someone's body. Domesticated guinea pigs are just as good at this, and black guinea pigs are particularly valued for this purpose. Unfortunately, it is also considered acceptable to cut the animal open to establish whether the cure has been effective.

Wild cavies grunt, gurgle, chatter, growl, and rumble to each other, to communicate. A pecking order will develop, where submissive cavies will lower their head, allowing a more dominant cavy to take his hierarchical position. This probably sounds familiar to anyone with a pair of guinea pigs, where one is always the dominant piggy!

When they mate, female cavies spend 60 to 70 days in gestation, before giving birth to a litter of babies. They usually have between one and four babies, who are born furry, and look like miniature cavies. They grow up fast and can become mature at two months of age.

Today's guineas pigs may originate from the first domesticated cavies, bred for food by South American tribes, around 7000 years ago. The Moche tribes in ancient Peru worshipped animals and frequently depicted guinea pigs in their artwork. Selective breeding began in 1200 AD, resulting in different varieties of domestic guinea pigs, many of which probably still exist today. Guinea pigs came to Europe with traders and were quickly adopted as a popular exotic pet. Queen Elizabeth I had one.

CHAPTER 13

SMALL FURRY PETS AS THERAPY

Stepney City Farm has a pilot study underway to see how Animal Assisted Activities can help old people in care homes. The scheme, called Furry Tales, involves staff and volunteers taking bantam chickens, guinea pigs and rabbits, to old people's homes and day centres. The residents enjoy non-judgmental companionship and physical contact, which keeps their minds active, and supports social interaction.

Ione Maria Rojas, Project Manager, explains: "The Furry Tales project at Stepney City Farm was inspired by my long-term interest in art therapies and elderly health. I volunteered in a couple of care homes running painting workshops. Then, having grown up in the countryside, I started volunteering at Stepney City Farm too, because living in London can be so intense. I found being around the Farm was beneficial to my wellbeing.

"There are people of all backgrounds at the farm and lots going on. The care homes are quite sterile in comparison, unable to offer much in the way of meaningful communication, due to their own limits on time and funds. I took a few small animals into a home that already had links to the Farm, and it just snowballed from there.

"It's been quite hard work turning a few informal visits into a regular commitment, but the Farm has been very enthusiastic about the idea. The feedback from the early visits enabled us to secure funding to do it properly, on a bigger scale, so we've been breeding our own animals specifically for this work. The funding goes towards animal care and housing, animal feed, vets' bills, transport, equipment and a salary for me to run it two days a week. I keep everything up to date and organise the volunteers - it keeps me very busy!"

The animals

"We use guinea pigs, rabbits, and Pekin Bantam chickens. They're all animals that will relax on people's laps and don't mind being handled. Many of our small furry pets have been born at the farm and raised with a lot of handling, so they're used to it. We know each animal's history and behaviour, and always take animals that are suited to the environment when we take them out to care homes and day centres.

"We have a black and white Abyssinian guinea pig named Jeanie who is very popular. A Furry Tales veteran, she is mum to three of our guinea piglets in training. She is friendly and calm and very patient, though nowadays we don't keep her out for so long as she gets tired. She was named after a resident at Silk Court Care Home, who formed a special bond with her. This lady doesn't tend to like group activities but she loves it when the animals arrive. She was delighted that Jeanie was named after her. Once, we had to take Jeanie off her lap, as the guinea pig was getting tired. This lady just smiled and said, 'That's OK, Jeans do get tired.' Everybody laughed.

"A recent addition to our team has been a ginger lion-haired rabbit, called Ron. We weren't sure about using him at first as we thought he could be a little temperamental. However, it seems he just needed to find his calling in life. He's a firm favourite with many residents, who love his lion-like mane. In a recent session, one man was very withdrawn and, though he smiled at us, he did not reach out to touch the animals and didn't try to say anything to us. As soon as we brought Ron out though, this man leapt out of his seat to stroke him and even started to sing! Each animal brings its own character to the project and you can just never tell how people will respond.

The process

"When we visit a home, we usually begin with the guinea pigs, moving onto rabbits, and then introducing chickens at the end. It's very hands-on. We teach people how to hold each animal so that none of them become distressed. Some of our animals will quite happily fall asleep on the residents' laps! People love them.

"Unless people are really keen to hold the animals right away, we handle them first, and approach the residents slowly, enabling them to get a good look at the animals and feel at ease around them. We'll hold a guinea pig in front of them and if the resident has a desire to have the guinea pig on their knee, we'll put the guinea pig on their lap. We do the same with the other animals. There's always a volunteer present with every animal, so the beneficiaries can stroke the animal and be as close, or as far away, as they want, for as long as they want. They have a plastic 'mole-skin' cover on their lap to catch any little 'accidents'!

"The animals' training is called 'animal socialising'. It involves getting them used to being with people and being handled. When the animals are very young, volunteers spend a lot of time with them, so they get used to being around people."

Stirring memories and nostalgia

"Some of the beneficiaries say that seeing the animals reminds them of their youth. It evokes old memories of those happy days. One said, 'It brings back memories of the animals we used to keep.'

"We've heard incredible stories of the elderly people's lives when they were young. It's interesting for the volunteers, because many of them are in their 20s and have not had this chance to hear about life in the 1940s and '50s on a personal level before.

"One volunteer told me she was really touched when the animals reminded one of the residents about his active past. He told her how he used to go dining and cycling all the time and he became very animated. It opened her eyes to how someone who is quite incapacitated from dementia and old age, once had a very full and active life.

"The whole experience promotes interaction because watching other people enjoying the animals can make those who are more reserved want to join in. The animals help to bring people out of themselves and those who are very withdrawn sometimes come to life, wanting to hold the rabbits and guinea pigs."

"At the moment, we go out to visit a care home once a month and we'd like to increase the frequency of visits and make it more regular. We also have fortnightly visits to the farm from elderly people who are suffering from isolation, we go out to day centres, and we have groups visit the farm from day centres, so we're pretty busy!

"I'm going to see Green Chimneys in the USA - a residential school for children with behavioural needs because they work with all different types of animals. It will be interesting to learn how they benefit from animal therapies, especially with the animals we use: guinea pigs, rabbits and chickens. I'm hoping to bring back what I learn to the UK so that we can improve our therapeutic offering here. It's remarkable how animal therapy has taken off around the world."

Day visits to the farm

"Sometimes people from day care centres come to the farm. They're often in their 60s or 70s, so they're more mobile than some of our other beneficiaries. They enjoy a farm tour, meet some of the larger animals, and feed the animals if they want to. It's a very sensory experience because they hear the cockerels and get the farmyard smells! It's much more stimulating in many different ways than taking an animal into a relatively sterile environment.

"When people visit the farm we get some very mixed and varied reactions. Sundial Care is one example of a group that has come many times and the residents are very enthusiastic. They recognise us as soon as the bus pulls up and they wave. They love to come back again and again.

"Other groups are more reserved. It's a change of environment for them and they're not sure what to make of it, so we move slowly before introducing them to the animals. We take them to an indoor space where they get a cup of tea and then we have a chat.

"We show them photos of the animals or eggs laid by the chickens. Eventually, we'll bring a few animals inside for them to see, and they can handle them if they want to. There are different staff around for them to talk to, and to help.

"When these visitors are ready to go and have a look around the farm yard, they can feed the guinea pigs and rabbits. We stand and watch the animals enjoying their food, and may spend quite some time there before we move on to see the field of chickens."

What the beneficiaries say

- Very interesting, very entertaining!
- I enjoyed today. Our favourite bit was the rabbits, we'd like to see the donkeys
- I certainly shall be telling people
- I have come here three times and I still haven't got tired of it. I want to come again and again... I liked being in touch with nature
- I have enjoyed the company... I feel like we're old friends and we just met today... Thank you for accepting me
- I love any chance to be with people
- It's bloody wonderful. I remember this place when there was nothing here – just a bombsite
- Thank you for bringing us these, it's not often we get to see this kind of thing
- The animals are lovely
- I used to love animals but nowadays I don't see any, except when we come to the farm
- I'm excited to see the chicken!
- It brings back memories of the animals we used to keep
- Very good, very enjoyable, especially the animals
- I enjoyed this time and last time – I'll come again next time
- I really enjoyed it. I like all the animals – thank you for having me

Thank You For Reading.

I Hope You Enjoyed The Book.

Please Consider Leaving A Review On Amazon.

Printed in Great Britain
by Amazon

52116782R00050